The Mommy Journal

The Mommy Journal

Letters to Your Child

by Tracy Broy

Andrews McMeel
Publishing, LLC

Kansas City

ISBN-13: 978-0-7407-2730-6
ISBN-10: 0-7407-2730-3

www.andrewsmcmeel.com

10 LEO 14 13 12

ATTENTION: SCHOOLS AND BUSINESSES

Andrews McMeel books are available at quantity discounts with bulk purchase for
educational, business, or sales promotional use. For information, please write to:
Special Sales Department, Andrews McMeel Publishing, LLC, 1130 Walnut Street,
Kansas City, MO 64106.

To Christopher and Kylie, who show me the meaning of true love every day. You are my life and I thank God for you.

To my parents, without whose love and support I truly don't know where I would be.

To my dear friend Becky Kubala, who has dedicated her life to helping women dealing with infertility reach their goal to become a mommy.

A portion of the profits from The Mommy Journal are being donated to Our Little Haven, a foundation set up to care for children who have been neglected, abused, or born drug-addicted or with HIV.

Dear Mommies,

I truly believe that the best thing I have ever done and ever will do is become a mom. The reason I created The Mommy Journal is because I wanted to share with moms a way to create and capture the memories of their children's lives. Let me explain.

When I was seven months pregnant I was sitting in the finished nursery rocking my unborn children and reading them a story. The twins began to kick each other and this overwhelming feeling of love rushed over me. I decided to write them a letter to capture my feelings and be able to look back on this special time in my life. I wanted to remember exactly how I was feeling. I sealed the letter and decided that I would give Christopher and Kylie this letter when they were older and could understand and have some insight into my feelings. I wrote another letter to them on the night they were born and have since written them a letter each night before their birthday.

When the twins were about six months old, my son was making this funny sound when he was getting ready to go to sleep. I remember thinking how cute it was and my mother said, "You think you will remember this, but you won't." I realized how true that was and decided to keep a journal of the things my children do and say. I don't journal every day because there are days (believe it or not) that are pretty uneventful. For the most part, however, I have plenty to write about.

I plan to give Christopher and Kylie these letters when they are adults and can truly appreciate them. I will be giving them a letter for each year of their childhood and hopefully give them a tradition they can pass down to their children. I feel I am giving them a part of myself, so that even when I am not around, they will always have a part of me with them.

Here's how to journal in your Mommy Journal. After you put the kids down, make yourself a hot cup of tea, relax in your favorite writing place, and think about what happened that day. Write down the funny things that were said or done, or maybe you had a trying day and you need to get your frustrations out. Please don't feel the pressure to journal every day. Life is sometimes overwhelming. Write when you can; it only has to take five minutes.

On the night before your child's birthday, go back through the journal and write a letter to your child based on what you've written in the past year. Seal it, put in your Keepsake Box, and get ready to capture the next year.

Happy journaling!

Tracy

P.S. I have included in the journal activities and songs that Christopher, Kylie, and I enjoy. I know there are days when I'm at a loss for something to do with them, so I thought I would share our favorites.

Date:————————

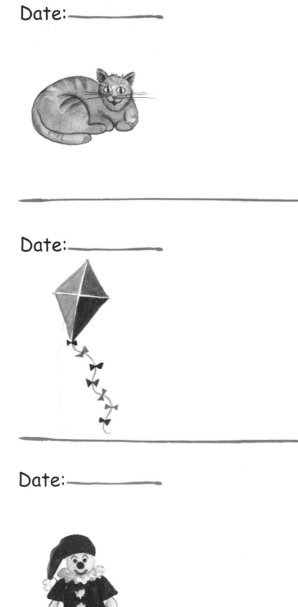

Date:————————

Date:————————

Date:————————

Loving a child is a
circular business. The
more you give, the more
you get, the more you
get, the more you give.
—Penelope Leach

Date:————————

Date:————————

Date:——————

Date:——————

Date:——————

Date:————

Hug your children every day and tell them how much you love them. Children who are loved learn to love others.

Date:————

Date:————

Date:—————

Date:—————

Date:—————

Date:————————

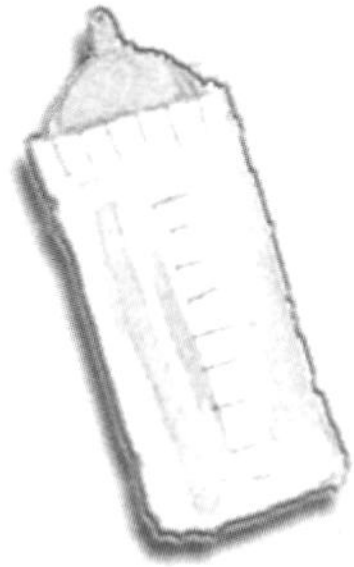

Date:————

Date:———— ————

Date:———— ————

Date:———— ————

Date:————————

A mother once asked a clergyman when she should begin the education of her child. "Madam," was the reply, "from the very first smile that gleams over an infant's cheek, your opportunity begins."
—Richard Whately

Date:————————

Date:————————

Date:———

Date:———

Date:———

Date: ————————

There's a time when you have to explain to your children why they're born, and it's a marvelous thing if you know the reason.
—Hazel Scot

Date: ————————

Date: ————————

Date:———

Date:———

Date:———

Date: _____

Date: _____

Date: _____

Date:———

Date:———

Date:———————

Take a picture of your newborn on the same day of each month for her first year. You will be amazed at the changes a month can make.

Date:———————

Date:———————

Date:————

Date:————

Date:————

Date:————————

Date:————————

Date:————————

Date:————

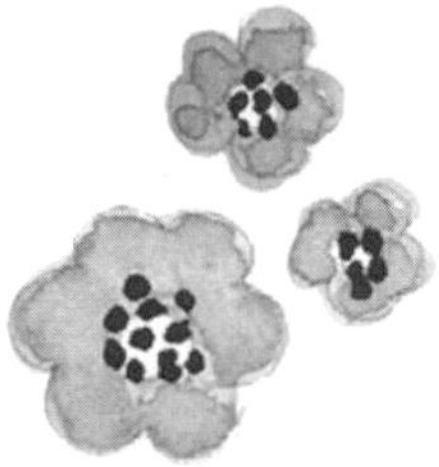

Date:————

Date:————

Date:———— ————

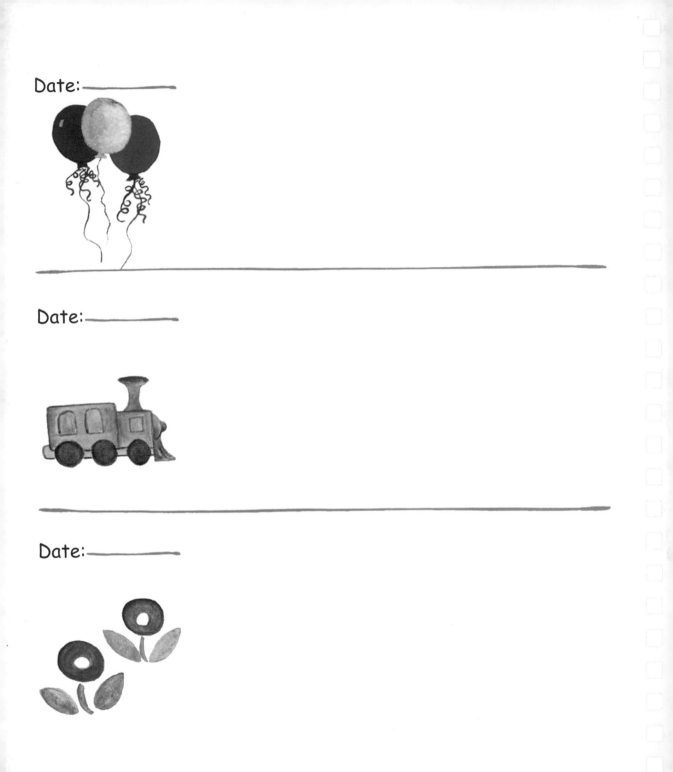

Date:————

Date:————

The Purple Cat Song

Out of the blue, riding in the car one day, my daughter Kylie started singing this song. She starts it off every time with a purple cat. It's a great song to sing while in the car because you can substitute what your children see outside. Here's how it goes:

Purple Cat, Purple Cat,

What do you see?

I see a car

Looking at me.

Car, Car

What do you see?

I see a school bus

Looking at me.

School Bus, School Bus

What do you see?

I see an airplane

Looking at me.

And so on, and so on . . .

Date:——————

Encourage your children to dream. They will become what you expect of them. If your expectations are high, what they expect of themselves will be high as well.

Date:——————

Date:——————

Date:————

Date:————

Date:————

Date:—————

Try baby massage on your infant if she is fussy or colicky. Your baby will love the feel of it. This also can be a special time for bonding.

Date:—————

Date:—————

Date:——————

Date:——————

Date:——————

Date:————

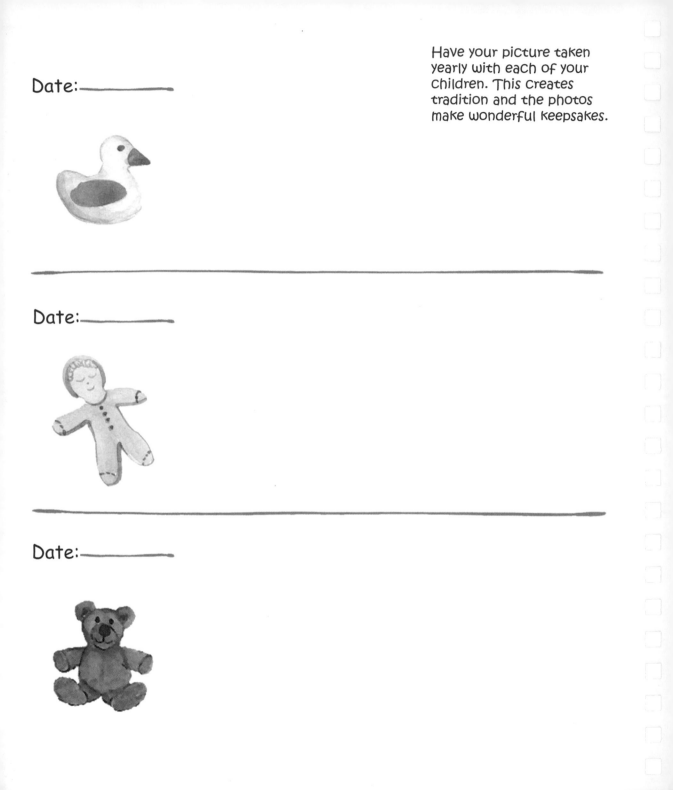

Have your picture taken yearly with each of your children. This creates tradition and the photos make wonderful keepsakes.

Date:————

Date:————

Date:————

Date:————

Date:————

Date:———————

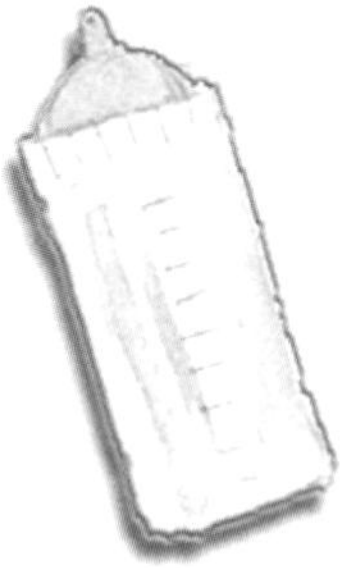

Date:———————

Date:———

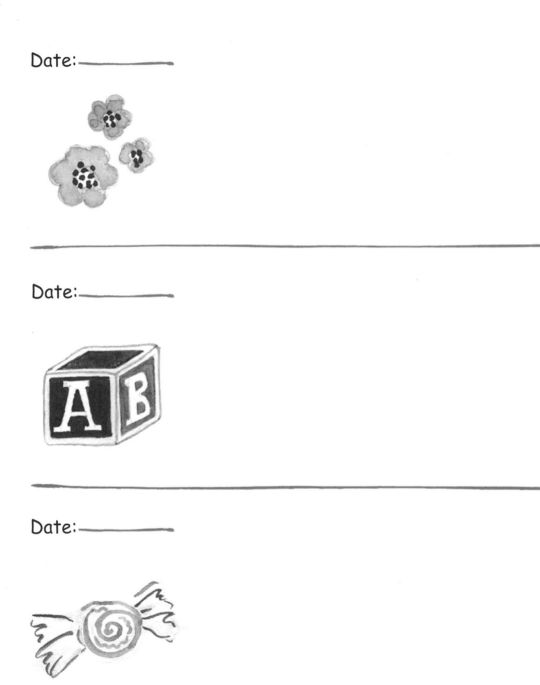

Date:———

Date:———

Date: _____

New moms, take some time for you . . . even if you don't have someone to watch the baby for an hour or so. Go for a nice walk with the baby in the stroller or in the baby holder. If it's winter, go to the mall. Just getting out will make you feel better.

Date: _____

Date: _____

Date:——————

Date:——————

Date:——————

Date:———————

A mother has perhaps the hardest earthly lot and yet no mother worthy of the name ever gave herself thoroughly for her child who did not feel that, after all, she reaped what she had sown.
—Henry Ward Beecher

Date:———————

Date:———————

Date:———

Date:———

Date:———

Date:————————

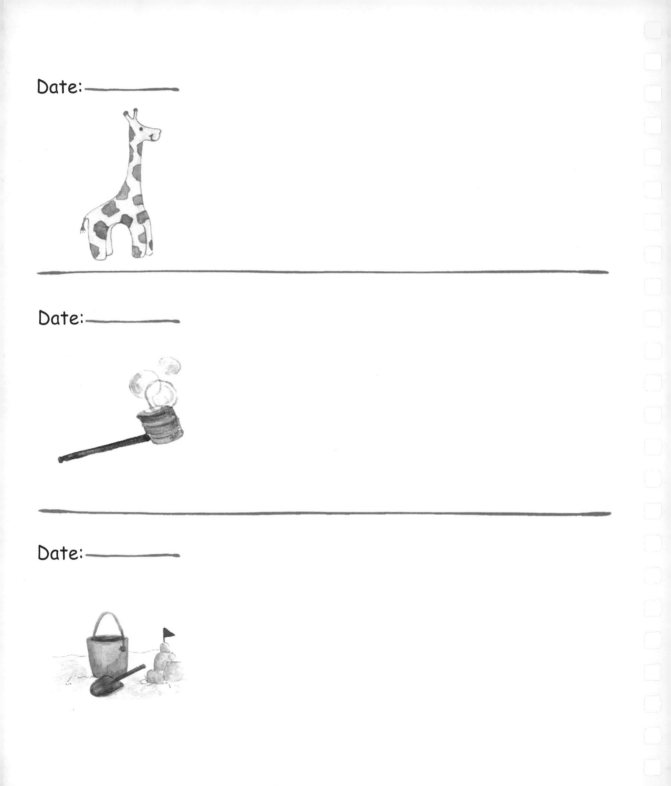

Date:————————

Date:————————

Date:———————

Date:———————

Date:———————

When your child does something wrong, instead of immediately yelling or disciplining, take a deep breath and count to ten. Children need to know they are loved, regardless of how many mistakes they make.

Date:———————

Date:———————

Date:———

Date:———

Date:———

Date:————————

Date:————————

Date:————————

Date:———————

Date:———————

Date:———————

Date:———

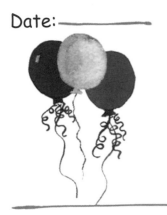

Date:———

Date:———

Mr. Alligator

Thanks to Mrs. Sinnett for teaching us this song.

Words:

Five little monkeys
   swinging from a tree,
Teasing Mr. Alligator,
   You can't catch me,
No, you can't catch me

Actions:

Swing your hand back
   and forth (five fingers up)

Point finger while shaking
   your head.

Along came Mr. Alligator
   Hungry as can be,
And he snapped that
   monkey right out of
   that tree.

Put hands together and
   move them in a zigzag
   motion as an alligator
   would while swimming.
Clap hands to make a
   snapping sound.

Following verses:

Four little monkeys . . .
Three little monkeys . . .
Two little monkeys . . .
One little monkey . . .

Date:————————

When people ask me what
I do, I always say I am
a mother first.
—Jacqueline Jackson

Date:————————

Date:————————

Date:—————

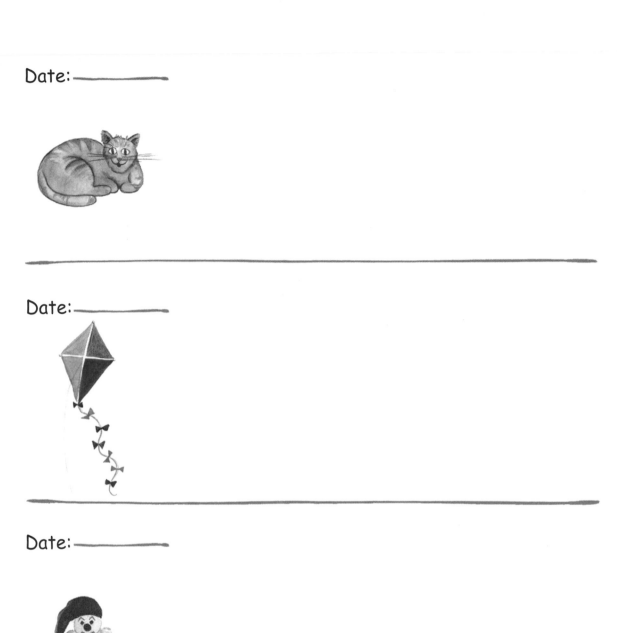

Date:—————

Date:—————

Date: ———————

Date: ———————

Date: ———————

Date:—————

———————————

Date:—————

———————————

Date:—————

Date: _____

Grocery shopping is sometimes stressful but can be fun. Make a list for your toddler and give him a crayon so he can pretend to check off the groceries. He will feel like he is part of the shopping and will want to stay in the cart.

Date: _____

Date: _____

Date:_____

Date:_____

Date:_____

Date: _____

Date: _____

Date:————————

Date:————

Date:————

Date:———————

A mother's love is patient and for giving when all others are forsaking, and it never fails or falters, even though the heart is breaking.
—Helen Steiner Rice

Date:———————

Date:———————

Date:———————

Date:————————

Date:—————————

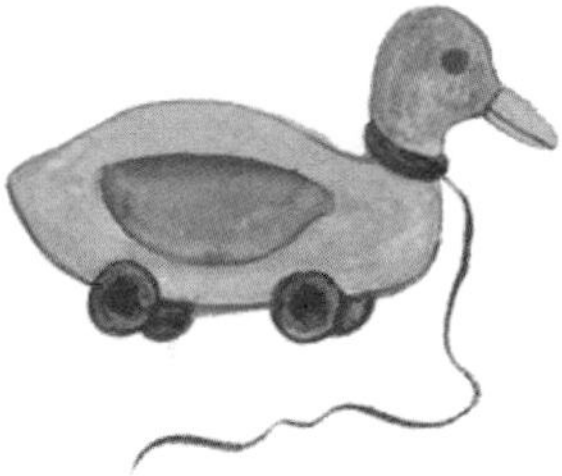

Date:————————

Bake a cake with your children. When it is cooled and frosted, cut a piece for each of you. Play a game by eating it with your hands behind your back. "Look, Mom, no hands!"

Date:————————

Date:————————

Date: —————

Date: —————

Date: —————

Date:———

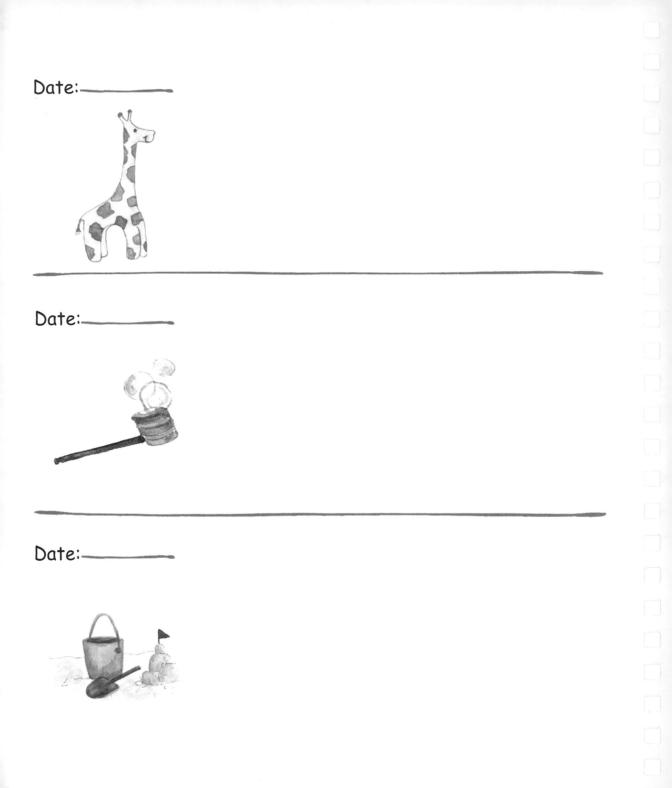

Date:———

Date:———

Date:——————

Date:——————

Date: —————

Date: —————

Date: —————

Date:———

Date:———

Date:———

Date: —————

Date: —————

Date: —————

Date:————

Date:————

Date:————

Date:———————

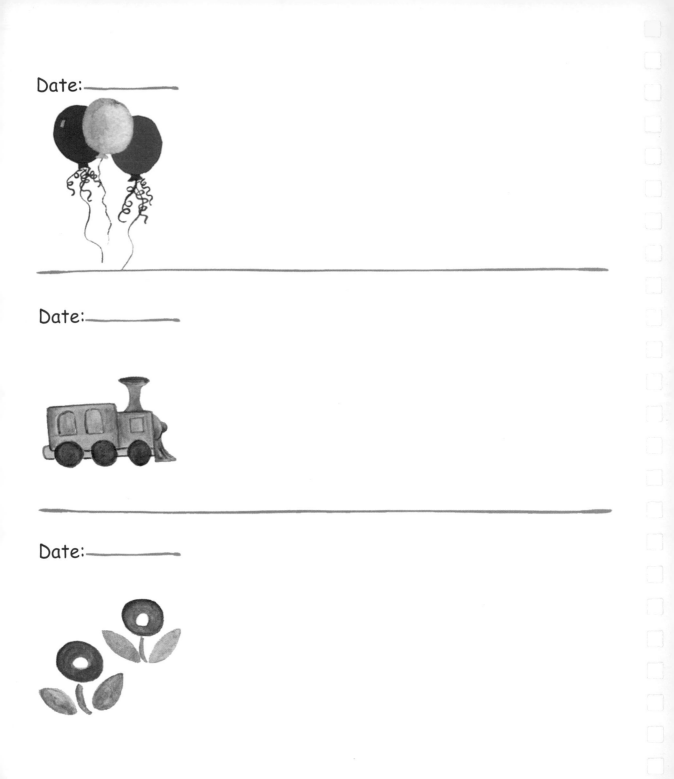

Date:————

Date:————

It's Your Birthday!

We all want to make our child's birthday as special as we can, so here are a few suggestions:

- Choose a book or books from this list and begin to read it the week before your child's birthday:

    Happy Birthday, by Gail Gibbons

    Benjamin's 365 Birthdays, by Judi Barrett

    The Secret Birthday Message, by Eric Carle

    Today Is Your Birthday, by P. K. Hallinan

- Have a plate that says "It's Your Special Day" and use it for everyone in the family on their birthday. We made ours at a local ceramic shop.

- Let your children bake and decorate a cake for themselves. When they are finished, let them eat it however they want!

- One month before your child's birthday, start a countdown on the calendar. Talk about what a birthday is and tell them the story about the day they were born.

Date: _____

If you want your child to accept
your values when he reaches his
teen years, then you must be worthy
of his respect during his younger days.
—James Dobson

Date: _____

Date: _____

Date: _____

Date: _____

Date: _____

Date: _____

Plant a garden with your children. It doesn't have to be very big. They will learn about different kinds of vegetables and flowers and how they grow. You may even get them to eat a vegetable or two!

Date: _____

Date: _____

Date:———————

———————————————————————————

Date:———————

———————————————————————————

Date:———————

Date: _____

On a beautiful, sunny day go out in the backyard with your children, lie down in the grass, and look up at the clouds in the sky. Talk about what is good in the world.

Date: _____

Date: _____

Date: _____

Date: _____

Date: _____

Date:————————

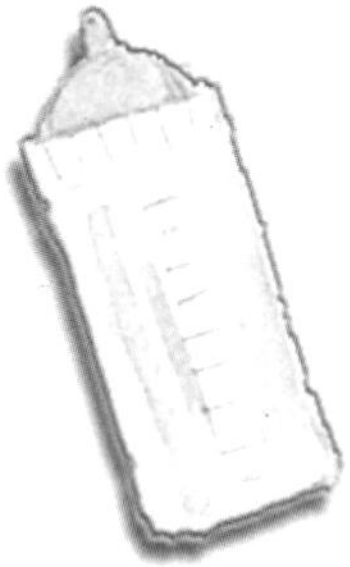

Date:————

Date:———————

———————————————————

Date:———————

———————————————————

Date:———————

Date:————————

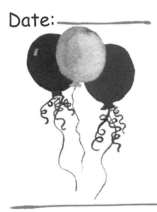

A happy childhood is one of the best gifts that parents have it in their power to bestow.
—Mary Cholmondeley

Date:————————

Date:————————

Date:——————

Date:——————

Date:——————

Date:————

Bake cookies with your children and give them to residents in a local nursing home. Children love to feel productive and cooking is a great way for them to create something. This also gives you a chance to instill in them the joy of giving to others.

Date:————

Date:————

Date:

Date:

Date:

Date: _____

Date: _____

Date: _____

Date:————————

Date:————

Date:—————

Date:—————

Date:—————

Date:————

Date:————

Date:————

Date: —————

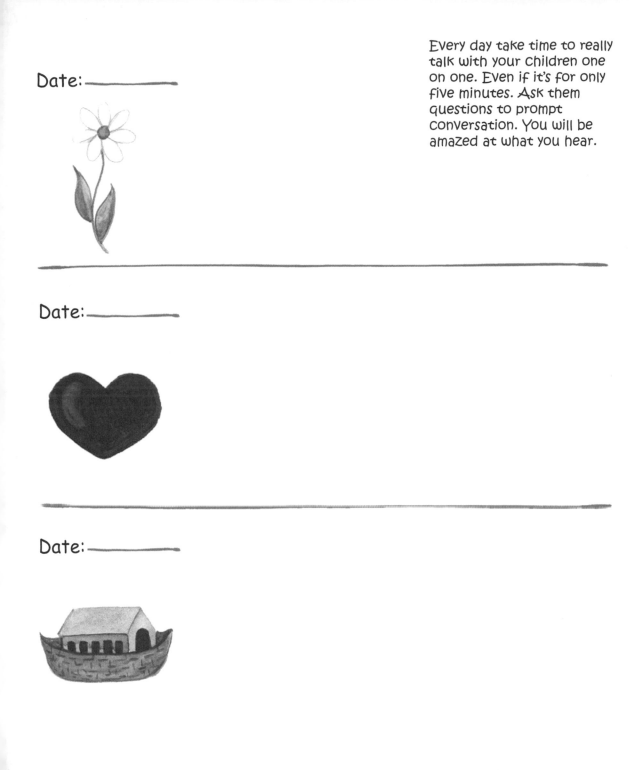

Every day take time to really talk with your children one on one. Even if it's for only five minutes. Ask them questions to prompt conversation. You will be amazed at what you hear.

Date: —————

Date: —————

Date:————————

Date:————————

Date:————————

Date: —————

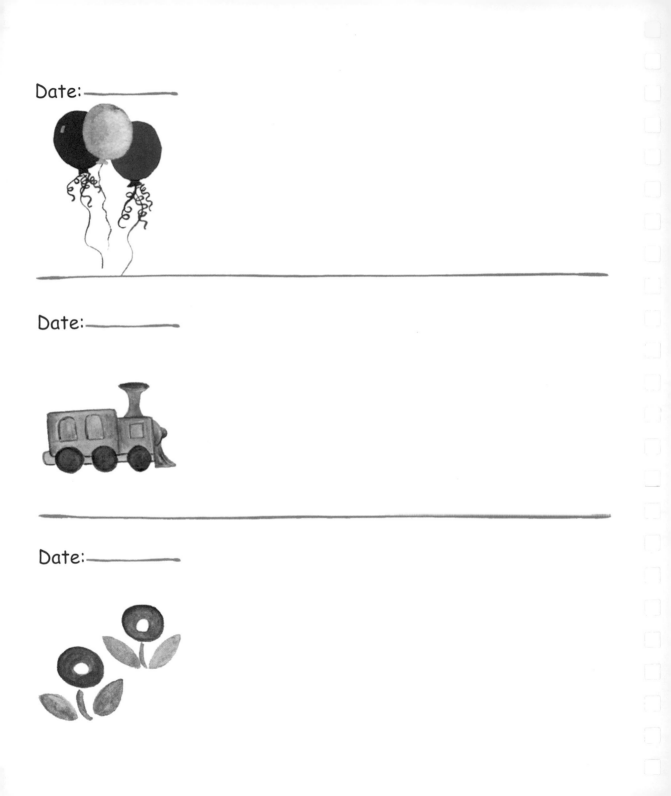

Date: —————

Date: —————

Homemade Play Clay

You can always buy Play-Doh at the store, but it's more fun to make. Keep several colors ready to play with on rainy days. For warm, sunny days, set up a child-size table and chairs under a shade tree and let the kids have their fun outside.

2 cups flour	2 TBSP. oil
1 cup salt	1 TSP. food coloring
1 TSP. cream of tartar	2 cups water

Mix ingredients together in a heavy saucepan and heat over medium heat, stirring constantly until dough leaves sides of the pan. Let it cool completely then knead out any bubbles. Store in plastic bags.

Date: _____

Date: _____

Date: _____

Date:———

Date:———

Date:———

Date: _____

When we set an example of honesty, our children will be honest. When we encircle them with love, they will be loving. When we practice tolerance, they will be tolerant. When we meet life with laughter and a twinkle in our eye, they will develop a sense of humor.
—Wilferd A. Peterson

Date: _____

Date: _____

Date:———————

Date:———————

Date:———————

Date:————

All that I am or hope to be, I owe to my mother.
—Abraham Lincoln

Date:————

Date:————

Date:————

Date:————

Date:————

Date: ————

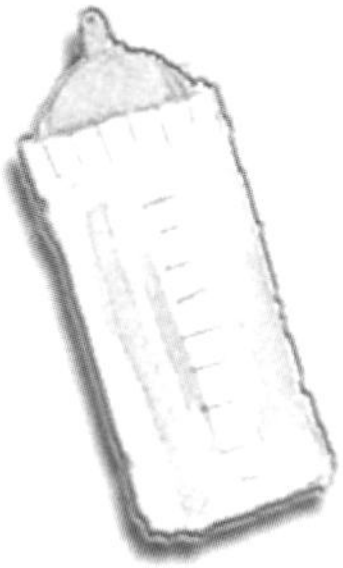

Date: ————

Date:————

Date:————

Date:————

Date:────────────

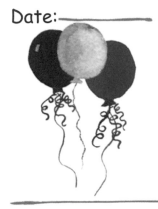

Date:──────────

Date:──────────

Date:———————

Date:———————

Date:———————

Date:————

My mother said to me, "If you become a soldier, you'll become a general: if you become a monk, you'll end up as the pope." Instead, I became a painter and wound up as Picasso.
—Pablo Picasso

Date:————

Date:————

Date:————

Date:————

Date:————

Date: ————————

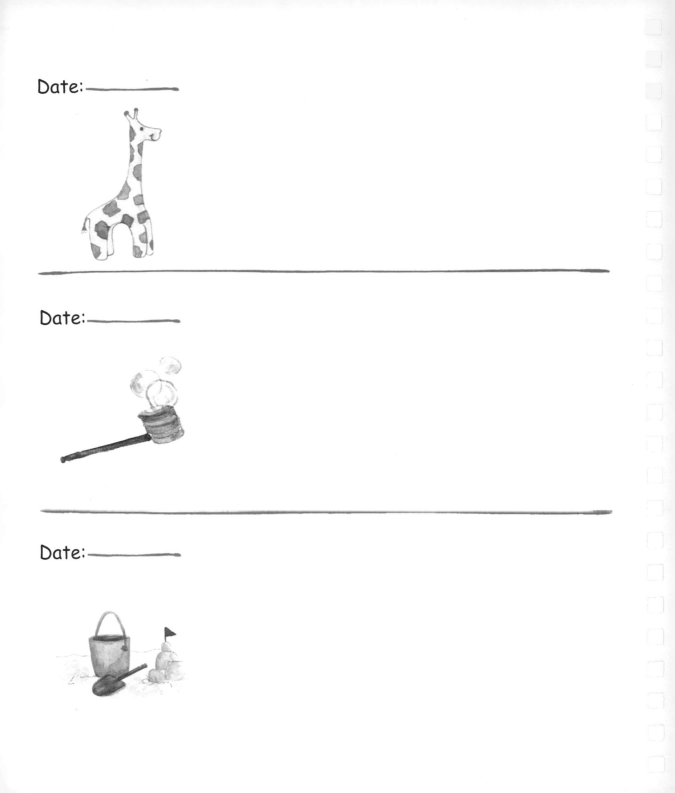

Date: ————————

Date: ————————

Date:———

Date:———

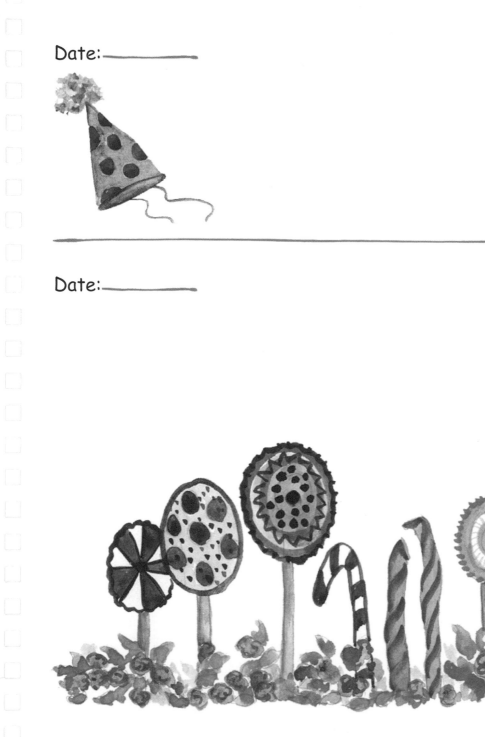

Date: ————————

Go to a ceramic shop and imprint your child's handprint on a mug or plate with her age underneath it. This makes a great gift or keepsake. While you are there, let her paint something on her own. She will feel a great sense of accomplishment.

Date: ————————

Date: ————————

Date:———————

Date:———————

Date:———————

If a child lives with approval,
he learns to live with himself.
—Dorothy Law Nolte

Date:——————

Date:——————

Date:——————

Date:———

Date:———

Date:———

Date:——————

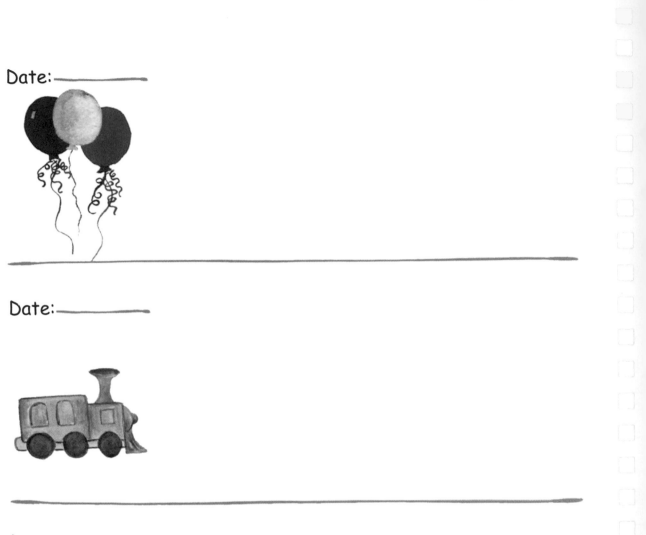

Date:——————

Date:——————

Let's Read Together

Here are some suggestions of books for you and your children to read together. Make storytime fun! On the weekends, we pop popcorn and for an hour or two before bedtime, we have a little reading party. These are some of our favorites:

Chicka Chicka Boom Boom, by Bill Martin Jr. and John Archambault
All by Myself, by Mercer Mayer
Goodnight Moon, by Margaret Wise Brown
Love You Forever, by Robert Munsch
Guess How Much I Love You, by Sam McBratney
Chicken Soup with Rice, by Maurice Sendak
Bye Bye Baby, by Janet Ahlberg
Twinkle, Twinkle Little Bug, by Katharine Ross
The Mitten, by Jan Brett
I Can! Can You?, by Peggy Parrish
On the Day You Were Born, by Debra Frasier
Little Bear (series of books), by Maurice Sendak
The Very Hungry Caterpillar, by Eric Carle
So Much, by Trish Cooke
Owl Babies, by Martin Waddell
Commotion in the Ocean, by Giles Andreae
Do You Want to Be My Friend?, by Eric Carle
Corduroy, by Don Freeman
Deep in the Forest, by Brinton Turkle
Cloudy with a Chance of Meatballs, by Judi Barrett
Mr. Rabbit and the Lovely Present, by Charlotte Zolotow
Anthony the Perfect Monster, by Angelo DeCesare
I Like Me, by Nancy Carlson
We are All Alike . . . We are All Different, by the Cheltenham
    Elementary School Kindergartners
Read-Aloud Rhymes for the Very Young, by Jack Prelutsky

Date:————————

Date:————————

Date:————————

Date:———————

Date:———————

Date:———————

Date: ———————

God sends children for another purpose than merely to keep up the race—to enlarge our hearts, to make us unselfish and full of kindly sympathies and affections.
—Mary Howitt

Date: ———————

Date: ———————

Date:————

Date:————

Date:————

Date: —————

A mother fills a place so great
that there isn't an angel in
heaven who wouldn't be glad
to give a bushel of diamonds
to come down here and take
her place.
—Billy Sunday

Date: —————

Date: —————

Date:———

Date:———

Date:———

Date: _____

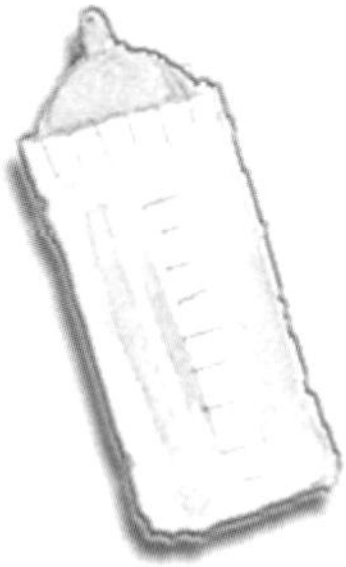

Date: _____

Date:———

Date:———

Date:———

Date:————————

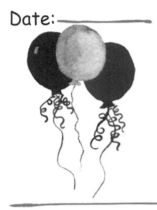

A child is a gift whose worth
cannot be measured except
by the heart.
—Theresa Ann Hunt

Date:————————

Date:————————

Date:——————

Date:——————

Date:——————

Children spell "love" T-I-M-E.
—Dr. Anthony P. Witham

Date:

Date:

Date:

Date:———

Date:———

Date:———

Date:————————

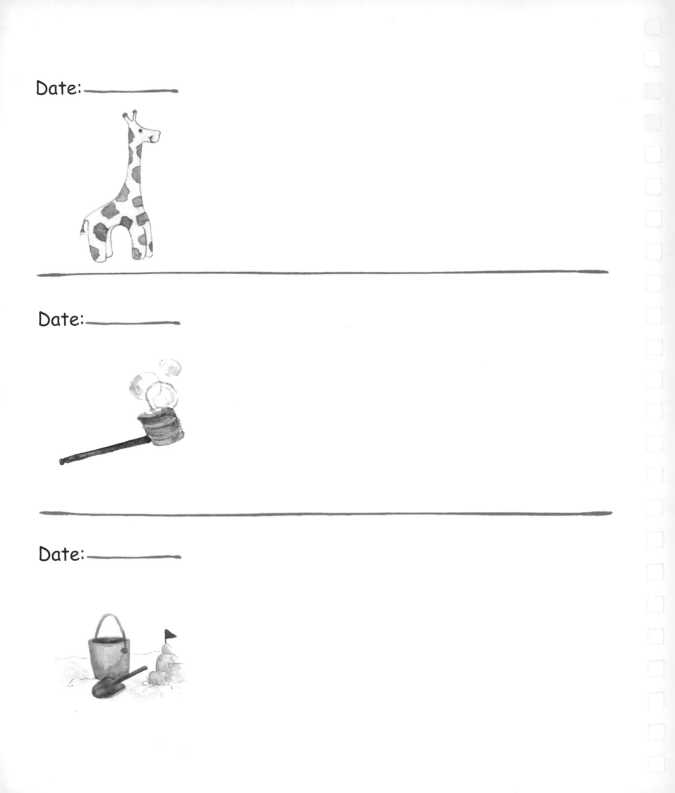

Date:————————

Date:————————

Date: ——————

Date: ——————

Date:———————

Date:———————

Date:———————

Date:———————

Date:———————

Date:———————

Date:————

Date:————

Date:————

Date:———————

Date:———————

Date:———————

Date:—————

Date:———

Date:———

Explore, Explore, Explore

On a pretty summer day when bugs are all around, go for an adventure into the woods. Pack a lunch, take a blanket, and be explorers. Here are a few things you might want to take along:

   A bug box for storing the little varmints you catch

   Tweezers for picking up those slimy creatures

   Bug spray, so you don't come home with any itchies

   A bug net

   A magnifying glass

   Towelettes

   A camera

   Food (for you, not the bugs!)

   Plenty to drink

Around Your Town . . .

Investigate all of the museums in your area and nearby places for your kids to go. You can call your local tourism bureau and have them send you information. It's fun to see what your city or town has to offer for your children to explore.

Have fun!

Date: ———————

Kind words can be short
and easy to speak, but
their echoes are truly
endless.
—Mother Teresa

Date: ———————

Date: ———————